IN
·1492·

BY

Jean Marzollo

ILLUSTRATED BY

Steve Björkman

SCHOLASTIC
HARDCOVER

SCHOLASTIC INC.
New York

For Shea Andrew Fumigalli
with love,
      Jean Marzollo

For Mom and Dad, who tolerated India ink on
the carpet as I explored a new world
           —Steve Björkman

Text copyright © 1991 by Jean Marzollo.

Illustrations copyright © 1991 by Steven Björkman.

Library of Congress Cataloging-in-Publication Data

Marzollo, Jean.
  In fourteen hundred ninety-two/by Jean Marzollo: illustrated by Steve
Björkman.
  p. cm.
  Summary: Rhyming text describes Christopher Columbus's first voyage to
the New World.
  ISBN 0-590-44413-1
  1. Columbus, Christopher—Juvenile literature. 2. America—Discovery and
exploration—Spanish—Juvenile literature.
[1. Columbus, Christopher. 2. Explorers. 3. America—Discovery and
exploration—Spanish.] I. Björkman, Steve, ill. II. Title.
E111.M35 1991
970.1'5—dc20
                                    91-100
                                      CIP
                                      AC

12 11 10 9 8 7 6 5 4 3 2 1   1 2 3 4 5 6/9

Printed in the U.S.A.   36

First Scholastic printing, October 1991

Book design by Laurie McBarnette

The illustrations in this book were painted in ink and watercolor.

Background Facts
About Christopher Columbus

Christopher Columbus was born in 1451 in Genoa, an important seaport and independent Italian republic. He went to sea when he was nineteen or twenty. In 1477 he and his brother, Bartholomew, were in Lisbon, Portugal. At that time, the Portuguese were trying to reach the Orient by sailing around Africa. Columbus thought he could find a shorter way by sailing due west. He asked the king of Portugal to give him three ships and pay for his experimental journey. The king said no.

In 1485 Columbus went to Spain. In 1486 he asked the Spanish king and queen to help him. Queen Isabella finally agreed to give Columbus ships, honors, titles, and a percentage of the trade he might find. And so, on August 3, 1492, Columbus sailed from Palos, Spain, to search for a quicker route to the Indies (the name then used for India, China, the East Indies, and Japan). He had three ships in his fleet: the *Santa María*, the *Niña*, and the *Pinta*. On October 7 his tired men thought they saw land. When they realized they hadn't, they wanted to go home. On October 10 they agreed to go on for three more days. On October 12 Columbus landed in the Bahamas on an island he named San Salvador. He thought he had reached the Indies so he called the natives "Indians," but what he actually had found was a land he had never heard of before.

Columbus died in 1506.

In fourteen hundred ninety-two
Columbus sailed the ocean blue.

He had three ships and left from Spain;
He sailed through sunshine, wind, and rain.

He sailed by night; he sailed by day;
He used the stars to find his way.

A compass also helped him know
How to find the way to go.

Ninety sailors were on board;
Some men worked while others snored.

Then the workers went to sleep;
And others watched the ocean deep.

Day after day they looked for land;
They dreamed of trees and rocks and sand.

October 12 their dream came true.
You never saw a happier crew!

"Indians! Indians!" Columbus cried;
His heart was filled with joyful pride.

But "India" the land was not;
It was the Bahamas, and it was hot.

The Arawak natives were very nice;
They gave the sailors food and spice.

Columbus sailed on to find some gold
To bring back home, as he'd been told.

He made the trip again and again,
Trading for gold to bring to Spain.

The first American? No, not quite.
But Columbus was brave, and he was bright.

We cheer for him and say hooray,
Especially on Columbus Day!